D1368742

FLYING MODELS

Brian Ward

Consultant: Henry Pluckrose

Photography: Chris Fairclough

FRANKLIN WATTS
New York/London/Toronto/Sydney

Copyright © 1992 Franklin Watts

Franklin Watts, Inc
95 Madison Avenue
New York, NY 10016

Ward, Brian R.
    Flying models / Brian Ward.
        p. cm. — (Fresh start series)
    Summary: Provides step-by-step instructions for making a variety
of flying models, including the basic paper airplane, stick glider,
and flying saucer.
    ISBN 0-531-14241-8
    1. Flying-machines—Models—Juvenile literature.   2. Hot air
balloons—Models—Juvenile literature.   3. Parachutes—Models—
—Juvenile literature.   [1. Airplanes—Models.   2. Flying machines—
—Models.   3. Models and modelmaking.]   I. Title.   II. Series: Fresh
start (London, England)
TL670.W34   1993
629.133'1—dc20   92-9908
                                                            CIP AC

Design: Edward Kinsey

Editor: Jenny Wood

Typeset by Lineage Ltd,
Watford, England

Printed in Belgium

Contents

Equipment and materials

This book describes activities that use the following:

Balsa cement (special glue, obtainable from model shops)

Balsa wood (used for most construction)

Brush (for applying paste)

Cardboard (postcard or greeting card weight)

Compass

Dressmaking or modeling pins (with large glass or plastic heads)

Felt-tip pens or watercolor paints (for decorating your models)

Gauze bandage for reinforcing wing joints

Length of flat chipboard or plywood (to use as a "building board," for cutting on and for building your models)

Matchboxes (empty)

Modeling clay, small nails, and paper clips (for balancing your models)

Oak tag

Pencil (HB) or fine-line marker

Pliers with cutting jaws, strong enough to cut through a paper clip (for making a hook to hold the motor in a rubber-powered model)

Polyethylene sheet

Propeller assembly 140mm-155mm (5.5"-6") diameter (bought ready-to-use from a model shop)

Protractor

PVC insulating tape, paper masking tape or transparent tape (for holding parts together while glue dries)

Rubber bands (for catapult launches)

Rubber motor, to drive a propeller (bought as lengths of strip rubber, 1mm thick and $\frac{3}{32}$" [2.4mm] wide)

Safety ruler (metric; hard plastic or steel)

Sandpaper (medium and fine grade)

Scissors

Sharp knife for cutting balsa wood (this can be a special balsa knife, or a handyman's knife with disposable snap-off blades)

Tracing paper or wax paper

Triangle

Water

White (PVA) glue, used for woodworking

To make successful flying models, you will need a number of simple materials. Some will be available around the home, while others can be bought inexpensively from a model store, art store, hobby shop, or stationer's.

Choosing balsa wood

The models in this book are built from balsa wood. This very light wood is available from hobby stores in convenient sheets of various sizes and thicknesses. Weight is the enemy of flying models so, as balsa is light, it is an obvious choice for construction. Balsa is also quite stiff and strong, if the proper grade is selected.

The size of a length of balsa wood is usually marked in inches and fractions of an inch, such as ³⁄₃₂″ x 3″. This measurement means that the piece of blasa in question is ³⁄₃₂″ (2.5mm) in thickness, and 3″ (75mm) wide. Balsa may also be sold in metric sizes which do not convert exactly to fractions, so use the nearest size to the one specified. This simple conversion chart will help you choose the correct size.

Standard balsa wood sizes	
Inches	**Millimeters**
¹⁄₃₂	0.75
¹⁄₁₆	1.5
⅛	3
³⁄₁₆	4.5

1 Balsa wood is supplied in 3-foot (0.91m) lengths, usually with the width and thickness printed on it.

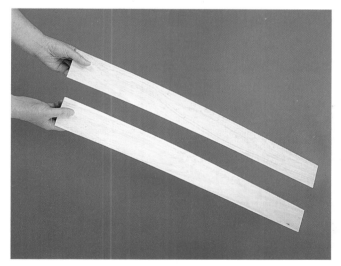

2 Take a stack of balsa wood from the rack in the store, and check through it carefully. Weigh each piece by gripping it at one end between finger and thumb, and holding it horizontally. It will be obvious if one sheet is much heavier or lighter than the others.

Look for the following characteristics when buying balsa:

1 Look for balsa with a straight grain. This means that the grain of the wood runs straight along the length of the sheet. Avoid balsa with grain that curves off at an angle, or that looks speckled. Balsa with hard streaks or patches in it will be hard to cut.

2 Buy only lightweight balsa. Even balsa of the same length and thickness does not all weigh the same. The balsa should not bend too much, neither should it be very soft and brittle.

3 Look along the length of the balsa sheet. It should be straight and flat – any curves or twists will mean that your model will not fly properly.

The models in this book are intended to be flown outdoors. In order to make them strong enough to withstand knocks and crashes, they all have wings made from ¹⁄₁₆″ (1.5mm) balsa sheet, and fuselages made from ³⁄₁₆″ (4.5mm) balsa. Models to be flown indoors, or outdoors in very calm conditions, can be built from much lighter materials. Although these will be fragile, they will fly better. Substitute ¹⁄₃₂″ (0.75mm) balsa for the ¹⁄₁₆″ (1.5mm) balsa wings and make fuselages from ¹⁄₈″ (3mm) balsa. (You must use ³⁄₁₆″ (4.5mm) balsa, however, for the fuselage of rubber-powered models, to provide sufficient strength.)

Marking out your plan

For a model to fly properly, it needs to be shaped accurately. For each model described in this book, you will find diagrams showing the parts that have to be marked on balsa wood and cut out.

Your first job is to transfer the shapes of the various parts of the model to balsa wood of the proper sizes. The diagrams for each new model show, as faint wavy lines, the direction of the grain on the wood. It is important to position the balsa wood so that the grain runs in the same direction as is shown on the diagrams (see picture 3).

3 Grain is indicated on the diagrams in this book by the use of faint, wavy lines.

4 Using a triangle and ruler, draw a grid of 10mm squares on a large sheet of tracing paper or wax paper.

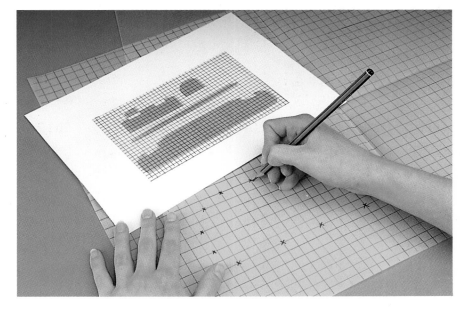

5 Now transfer the diagram onto your paper pattern, by counting the number of squares and marking each square in the corresponding position on your paper grid. It is not necessary to mark every position.

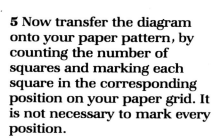

6 Lay the pattern over a sheet of balsa and push two pins through to keep the pattern from sliding. Using a dressmaking pin, prick around the outline of the drawing into the balsa.

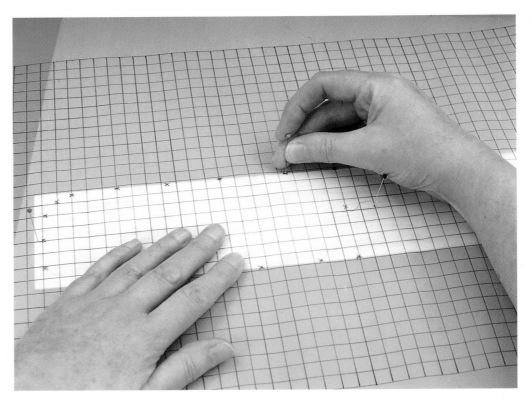

7 When you remove the pattern, you will see the pinholes. Connect them with a smooth pencil or pen line, then use this line to guide you when you cut out the parts.

Cutting and shaping

To cut balsa wood cleanly, you should use a very sharp knife. You can buy special modeling knives with replaceable blades, but these can be rather expensive. The cheapest and most effective type of knife has blades that are scored across so sections of blade can be broken off when they get blunt. The blunt section is replaced by a new and sharper section of blade which slides out of the handle.

8 Be careful when breaking off a blunted section of blade. It will still be very sharp and could cut you badly if mishandled, so follow exactly the directions provided with the knife. The part you break off must be disposed of carefully so that it does not injure anyone.

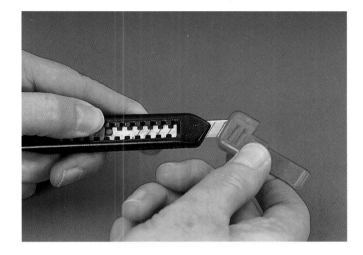

9 It may be difficult to cut right through a thick piece of balsa, as the knife blade may "wander" away from the straight steel edge. You may need to make several shallow cuts. Always cut away from the grain of the wood, otherwise the blade may dig in to the wood and spoil the line of the cut.

Except when carving a shape or cutting a curve, you should always cut balsa sheet against a straight metal edge such as the edge of a steel safety ruler. Lay the piece of balsa on the flat surface of your "building board, and hold it down firmly with the steel ruler. Hold the knife upright so it cuts squarely, and try to cut right through the wood with a single cut.

Sandpapering

You will need to smooth balsa parts with sandpaper, even if you have cut them very carefully. Use medium-grade sandpaper to shape the outline of the parts. Finer grade sandpaper will leave the wood smooth and ready to decorate.

Sanding produces lots of messy dust, which is unpleasant when inhaled. You can buy cheap filter masks, but it is easier to do your sanding outdoors.

10 Obtain a small, flat block of wood. Tear off a strip of sandpaper and wrap it around the wood. Use this sandpaper block to shape the balsa. For curved parts of a model, such as the one shown here, cut them oversized, and then shape them properly with sandpaper.

Gluing

For most glued joints, you should use balsa cement. This special glue dries quickly and strengthens the balsa wood. Do not use too much cement on the joint, but spread it evenly with a piece of scrap balsa or a wooden matchstick.

Allow plenty of time for cement to dry before you handle the model (usually about half an hour). Trim away any blobs of cement with your knife, and clean up the glue joint with sandpaper.

11 After gluing, press the pieces of wood together. While the cement is drying, push dressmaking pins through the joint to hold it steady. You can hold some joints together with tape, depending on the shape of the parts you are joining.

12 Once the cement has dried, you can add strength by running a line of cement along the outside of the joint. This is particularly useful where the wings, tail plane and fin join the fuselage.

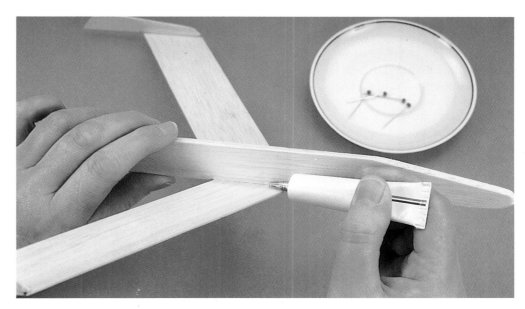

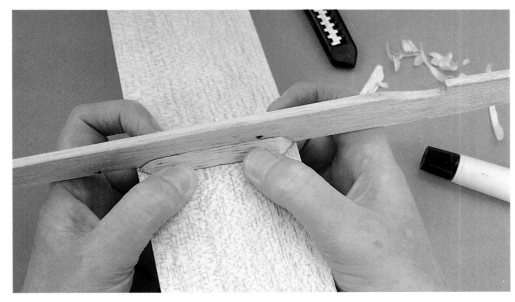

13 The joint will be even stronger if you glue a length of triangular balsa fillet along the line of the joint. You may need to carve the triangular balsa so it fits snugly in the dihedral angle.

The joint between the two halves of a wing needs to be particularly strong. The edges to be joined should be preglued. A thin coat of cement is left to dry without joining the wing halves. Once this has dried thoroughly, give the joint areas another coat of cement and pin or clamp the wing halves while they dry.

Another way of strengthening wing joints is to add gauze bandage reinforcement (see picture **14**).

14 Cut a strip of bandage about ¾" wide, and long enough to wrap around the wing root with a small overlap. Stick this to the wing root, using PVA glue. Using your fingertip, rub the glue over the joint area then, starting about ⅛" in from the underside of the front of the wing, wrap the bandage around. Once the bandage is in place, you can rub more glue over it, until it is well soaked and pressed down smoothly. Let it dry overnight.

15 You can also use PVA glue or cement to harden wing tips so they do not get dented in hard landings. Rub the cement into the wood with a fingertip, so that it soaks in.

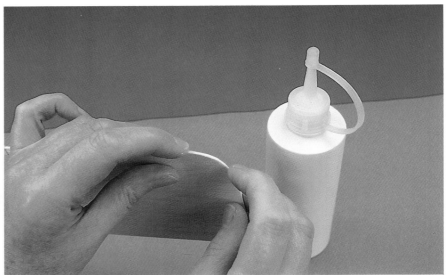

Remember to put the cap on the cement tube or glue bottle when you have finished, or seal the nozzle with a pin. You can clean cement and PVA glue from your fingers by soaking them in warm soapy water and picking off the adhesive.

Decorating your model

Lightness is essential for successful flying, so don't overdo the decoration! The best way of decorating models is to use felt-tip pens, which will not add any measurable weight.

To make an elaborate color scheme, you will need to seal the porous surface of the balsa wood. Prepare a mixture of one teaspoonful of PVA glue, thoroughly mixed with half a cup of cold water, and apply this with a soft paste brush, very thinly, over the area you want to decorate. Paint the mixture on both sides of the balsa, or the wood will warp. Once the sealing mixture has dried (between one and two hours), rub the model over lightly with fine sandpaper until it feels smooth.

16 When applying color with a felt-tip pen, press lightly and keep the pen moving. If you press too hard, the pen tip may score the wood. This looks bad and weakens the balsa.

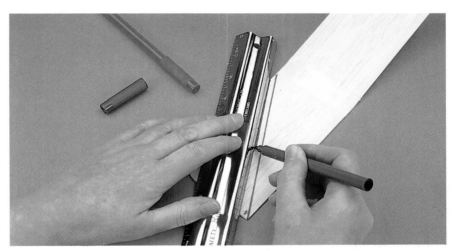

17 If you have sealed the surface of the balsa wood, you can use thin coats of watercolor paint to decorate your model. The sealed surface keeps the paint from soaking into the wood.

Balancing your model

On the diagrams in this book, you will see a small symbol [↑] marked on the side of the fuselage. This is the balance point, or center of gravity (CG), which must be in the right place if the model is to be stable in flight.

18 To check the center of gravity, make a hole through the fuselage with a small nail, and push through a toothpick or matchstick at right angles to the fuselage. If you support the toothpick or matchstick on your fingers, you will be able to see if the model balances nose-up or nose-down.

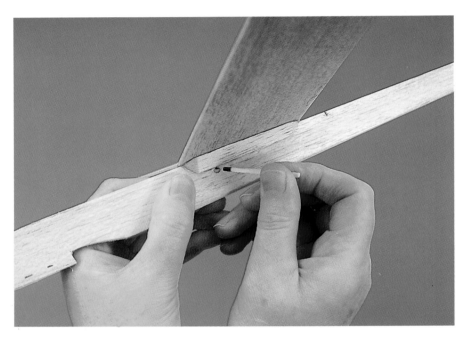

19 Add modeling clay or paper clips, or push small nails into the lighter end of the fuselage until it balances level or slightly nose-down. Then remove the matchstick.

Flying and trimming
The following notes will help you
make your model fly correctly.
They apply to all the models in
this book. Wait for a calm day,
with little or no wind.

20 Hold your model
firmly, just behind the
center of gravity, and
pointing slightly nose-
down.

21 Launch the model
smoothly and steadily,
with a firm push,
rather than throwing
it. Do not throw the
model up into the air
at this stage. The
model should travel
straight and level,
landing about 16 feet
in front of you.

22 If the model dives
into the ground, bend
the trim tabs on the
tail plane.

23 If the model climbs
at first, then dives into
the ground, add more
weight to the nose.

24 If the model turns
sharply, bend the trim
tab on the wing on the
outside of the turn up.

25 Try launching the
model a little harder,
and make sure that it
still performs
properly. Now bend
up the trim tab on the
left wing to make the
model circle gently to
the left. If you tilt the
model to the right as it
is launched, it will first
turn right, then left.
Launching hard and
straight ahead usually
causes a stall or a
complete loop, which
may be followed by a
damaging crash.

26 Once you are
satisfied that the
model is properly
trimmed, try
launching it by
catapult. Use a large
rubber band held
firmly in your left
hand, and caught in
the notch beneath the
fuselage. Launch the
model slightly upward
and tilted to the right.
NEVER DIRECT IT
TOWARD ANYONE.

Chuckie

This is a hand-launched, or "chuck," glider which makes a simple introduction to flying models. It is a tough model, which can be catapulted into the air for longer flights.

You will need a sheet of balsa ³⁄₁₆" (4.5mm) thick, a sheet of balsa ¹⁄₁₆" (1.5mm) thick, dressmaking or modeling pins, a pencil or fine-line marker, a metal ruler, a woodworking knife, medium-grade and fine sandpaper, a triangle, tape, some polyethylene sheet, a building board, an empty matchbox, balsa cement, cardboard, scissors, and modeling clay.

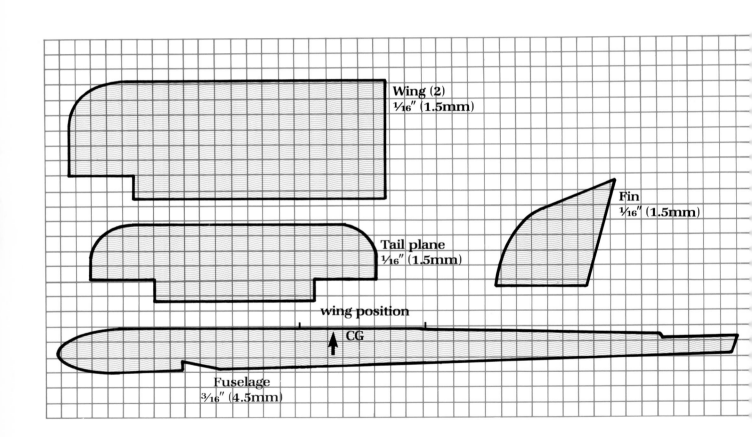

Wing (2)
¹⁄₁₆" (1.5mm)

Fin
¹⁄₁₆" (1.5mm)

Tail plane
¹⁄₁₆" (1.5mm)

wing position

CG

Fuselage
³⁄₁₆" (4.5mm)

1 Start by making the fuselage. Mark out, on a piece of ³⁄₁₆″ (4.5mm) balsa, a rectangle 430mm long x 30mm wide. Draw a line from the front of the fuselage to the tail, so it tapers to a depth of 12mm. Draw smooth curves to round off the nose shape (the exact shape is not important), and mark out a catapult notch in the underside, 80mm back from the nose.

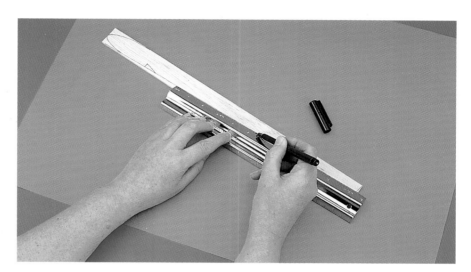

2 Using the knife and the metal ruler, cut out the shape of the fuselage. Use first medium-grade then fine sandpaper to smooth the curved outlines. Round off the undersurface of the fuselage, but leave the top edge quite flat where the wings and tail plane will be fitted.

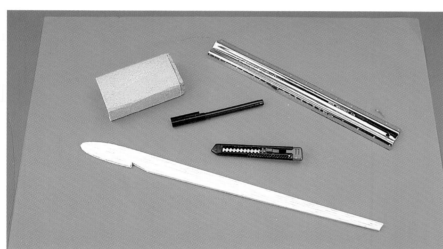

3 Mark a point 50mm in from the back of the fuselage, and cut out a tapered section where the tail plane will fit (see diagram). The front of the cut-out must be exactly 1.5mm deep.

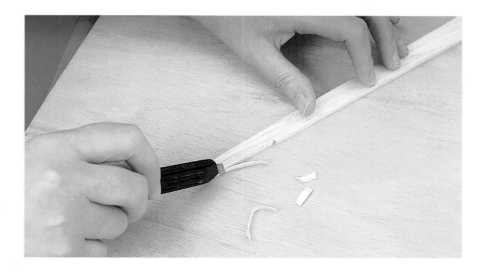

4 Make the wings from two pieces of ¹⁄₁₆″ (1.5mm) balsa, 75mm wide x 200mm long. Use the triangle to make sure that you have cut the wing roots at an exact right angle. Using tape, temporarily affix the two pieces together.

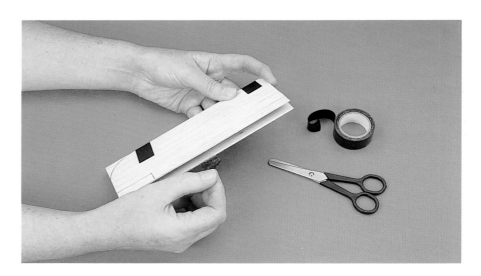

5 Cut out the wing shape, then carefully cut the wing tips to a curved shape.

6 Cut the tail plane from ¹⁄₁₆″ (1.5mm) balsa, 50mm wide x 180mm long. Round off the tips with sandpaper, and then cut out the fin.

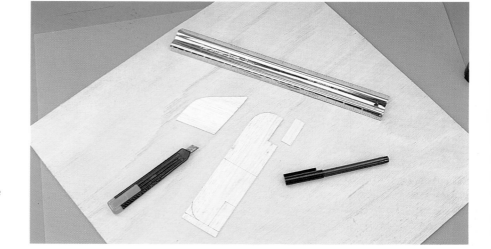

7 Place the polyethylene sheet over your building board, and pin one wing down flat. Stand the matchbox on end so that it will support the other wing tip, and apply cement to the wing root. Pin the other wing in place, with the tip supported on the matchbox, and leave until the glue has set.

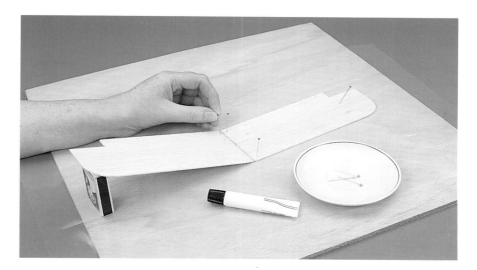

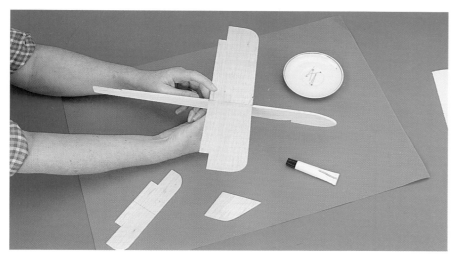

8 Cement the wing to the top of the fuselage, with its front, or leading edge, 150mm from the nose. Pin it in place and, while looking from the front, make sure that it sits squarely on the fuselage. Glue balsa fillets to strengthen the wing joint.

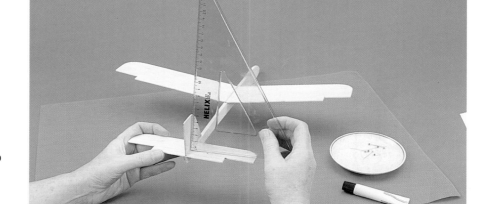

9 Glue and pin the tail plane into place, using the triangle to make sure it is properly positioned. Pin and glue the fin, again using the triangle.

10 Glue small cardboard trim tabs onto the wings and tail plane. Check that your model balances properly, using modeling clay to adjust the center of gravity (see page **14**).

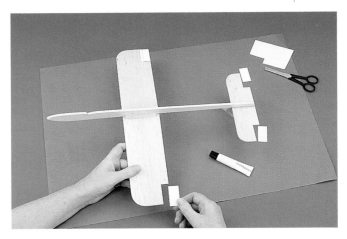

11 The finished model.

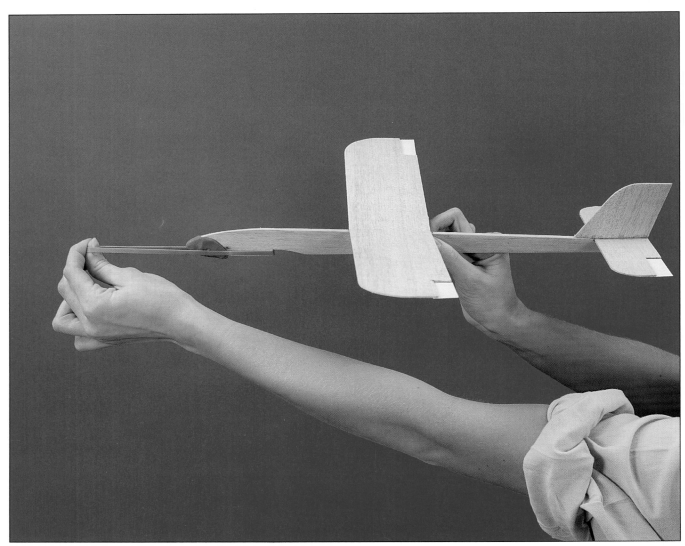

Saucerer

The flying saucer is an example of a tail-less aircraft, in which the function of the tail plane or stabilizer is carried out by the upward curve of the rear part of the wing. this type of model is strong and stable and, because of its shape, is unlikely to be damaged in a hard landing.

You will need a sheet of balsa ³⁄₁₆″ (4.5mm) thick, balsa ¹⁄₁₆″ (1.5mm) thick, a pencil or fine-line marker, a metal ruler, a woodworking knife, medium grade and fine sandpaper, tape, scissors, balsa cement, a compass (or a plate to draw around), PVA glue, water, a paste brush, and colored felt-tip pens or watercolor paints to decorate your model.

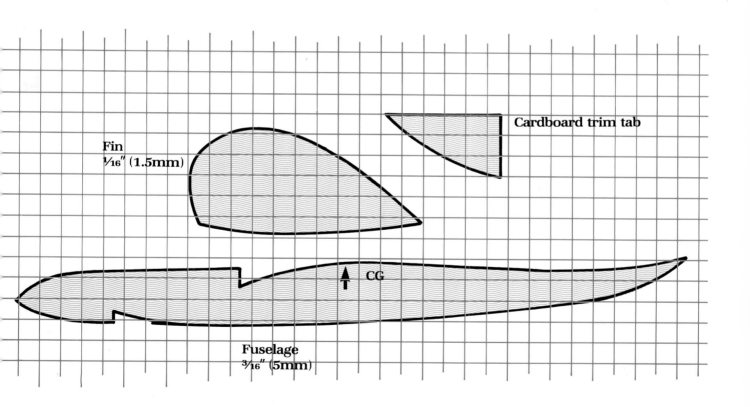

Fin
¹⁄₁₆″ (1.5mm)

Cardboard trim tab

CG

Fuselage
³⁄₁₆″ (5mm)

1 Cut the fuselage from ³⁄₁₆″ (4.5mm) balsa. You will need a piece 30mm wide x 300mm long. Refer to the diagram, then carefully transfer the outline to the balsa, being particularly careful with the curved cutout where the wing fits. Cut out along the lines you have marked.

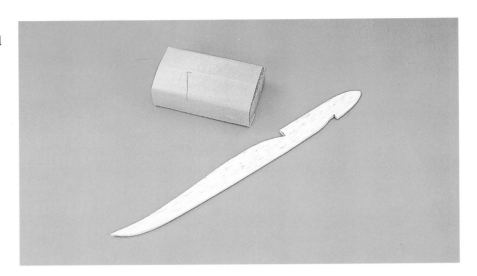

2 Cut out three pieces of ¹⁄₁₆″ (1.5mm) balsa. Each piece should be 75mm wide x 210mm long. Lay these pieces together side by side, and tape over the joints on one side only. Fold the wood back and apply glue to the edges of each joint, then lay flat to dry.

3 You will now have a piece of balsa 210mm x 210mm. Find a plate or dish of about this size to draw around, or use the compass to mark a circle. Cut out the circular wing. Cut out the area for the trim tabs.

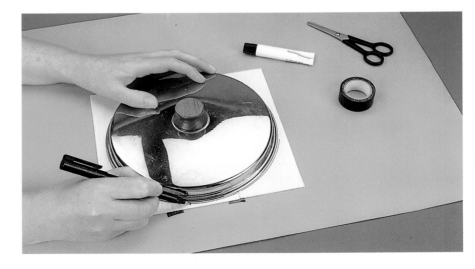

4 This is a particularly easy model to decorate. Give the wing a thin coat of thinned PVA glue as described on page 13, then use watercolor paints or felt-tip pens to decorate it. Decorate before attaching the wing on the fuselage. Coat both sides with the glue mixture, to prevent warps.

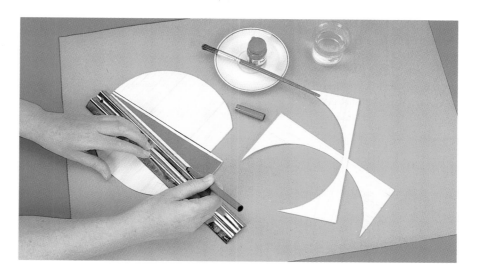

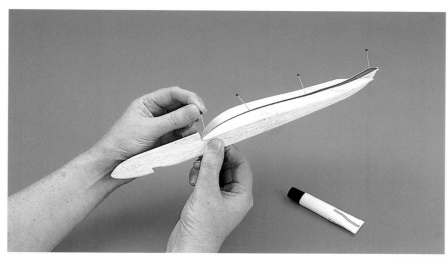

5 Cement the circular wing into place, making sure it fits squarely on the fuselage. Hold it in its curved seating with pins. The grain of the wood must be at right angles to the fuselage.

6 Cement a small, wedge-shaped scrap of ³⁄₁₆″ (4.5mm) balsa to the front of the wing where it joins the fuselage. Cut and sand it so it fits smoothly to the shape of the model.

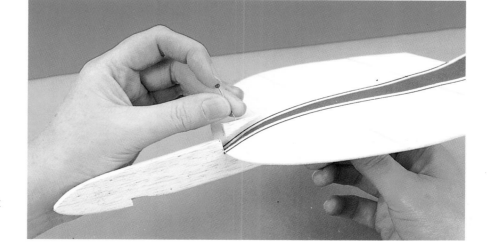

7 Mark out, cut and cement on the fin. You can make the fin any shape you like, as long as it is about the same size as the one shown.

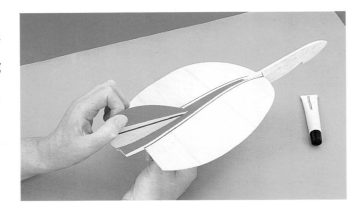

8 Attach cardboard trim tabs as shown, and balance the model. If the Saucerer dives when you fly it, bend up both trim tabs to correct the dive. Use the trim tabs as described on page 15 to correct or produce a turn.

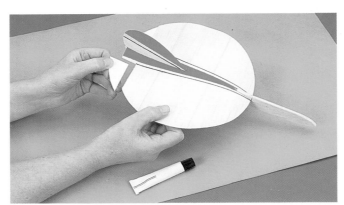

9 The finished model.

Concarde

This tail-less, or "delta-winged," model is small and easy to make. You will need a small length of balsa either ³⁄₁₆″ (4.5mm) or ⅛″ (3mm) thick for the fuselage, some balsa ¹⁄₁₆″ (1.5mm) thick and thin cardboard for the wing, a metal ruler, a woodworking knife, sandpaper, a sheet of oak tag, a pencil or fine-line marker, cardboard, scissors, and balsa cement.

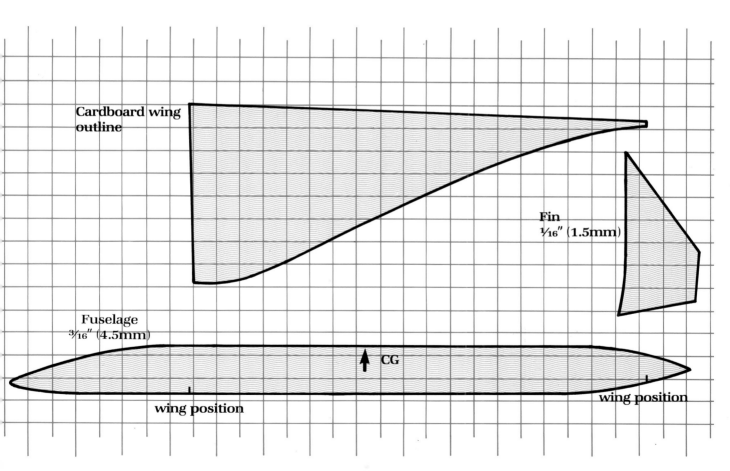

Cardboard wing outline

Fin ¹⁄₁₆″ (1.5mm)

Fuselage ³⁄₁₆″ (4.5mm)

CG

wing position

wing position

1 Cut a strip of balsa for the fuselage, 290mm long x 20mm wide. Carefully mark out the shape of the nose and tail, and cut out the curved shapes shown. Cut out the fin.

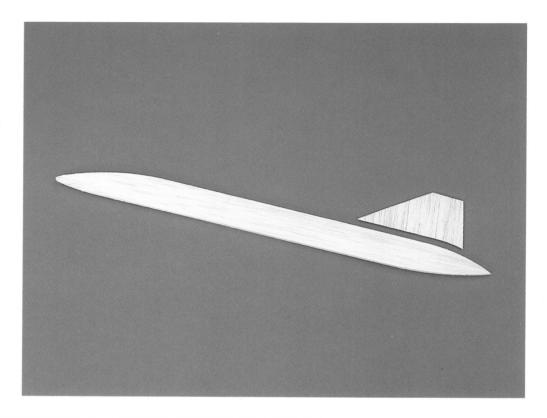

2 Fold the paper lengthwise, and copy the wing shape onto it. Cut around the curved outline, and unfold the paper. Use this as a pattern, drawing around it onto a piece of cardboard to mark out the wing.

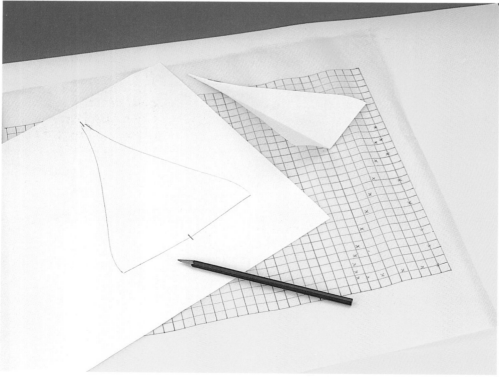

3 Cut out the wing with scissors.

4 Cement the cardboard wing and balsa fin into place, and add a small length of scrap balsa underneath, to provide a finger grip when you launch the model. Balance the model carefully.

5 Trim Concarde like the Saucerer, but bend the trailing edge of the wings up or down instead of using trim tabs.

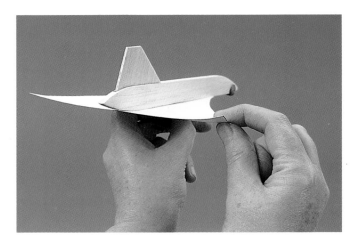

6 The finished model.

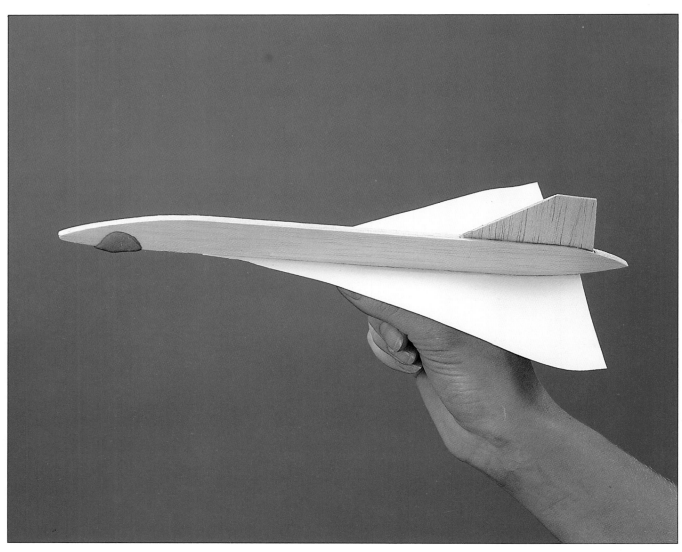

This model is powered by a rubber motor. If constructed lightly and accurately it will produce long flights, so it is best to fly it in an open field. You will need balsa $\frac{3}{16}''$ (4.5mm) thick, balsa $\frac{1}{16}''$ (1.5mm) thick, a pencil or fine-line marker, a metal ruler, a woodworking knife, sandpaper, balsa cement, some polyethylene sheet, a building board, empty matchboxes, gauze bandage, PVA glue, a triangle, dressmaking or modeling pins, a paper clip, pliers, rubber strip for the motor, a 140mm-155mm (5½"-6") propeller assembly, and cardboard.

You can obtain the rubber strip and propeller assembly from a specialty model or hobby store. There are several different types of propeller assembly, so you will have to explain your requirements and ask for the storekeeper's advice. Some of the propellers vary slightly in the way they are assembled and attached, so you might need to make some small alterations to the model. These will usually be quite simple, but if not, ask for advice.

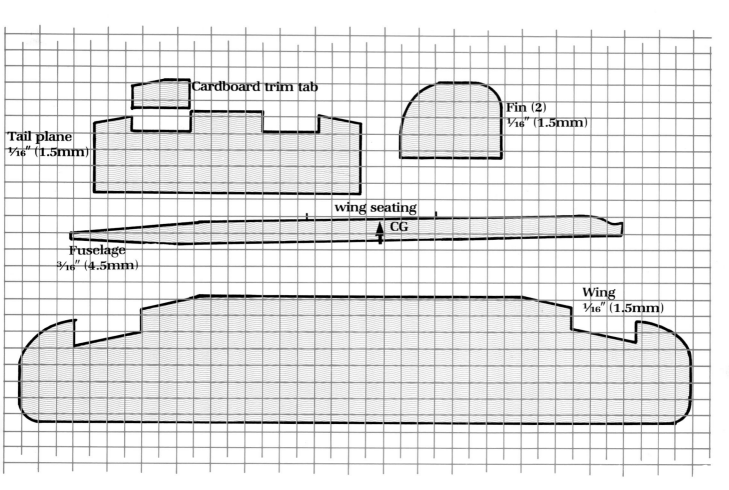

Cardboard trim tab

Tail plane
$\frac{1}{16}''$ (1.5mm)

Fin (2)
$\frac{1}{16}''$ (1.5mm)

wing seating

CG

Fuselage
$\frac{3}{16}''$ (4.5mm)

Wing
$\frac{1}{16}''$ (1.5mm)

1 Cut the fuselage from ³⁄₁₆″ (4.5mm) blasa 330mm long x 12mm wide. Taper the rear of the fuselage as shown, taking particular care to make the taper on the underside accurate, where the tail plane will be affixed. Carefully cut and sand the front of the fuselage, until it fits into the socket on the propeller assembly. It should be a tight push fit, and note that the propeller shaft should point slightly downward and to the right of the line of the fuselage. This downthrust prevents the model from zooming upward under power. Cement the propeller assembly into place.

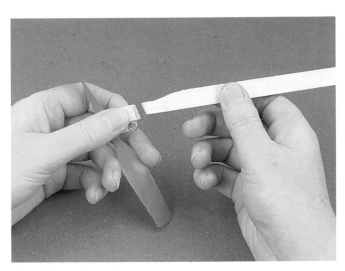

2 Mark out the wings on ¹⁄₁₆″ (1.5mm) balsa. Draw a rectangle 400 mm long x 75mm wide. Measure in 100mm from each end, and mark lines at right angles to the leading edge. Draw the tapered and curved wing tips as shown.

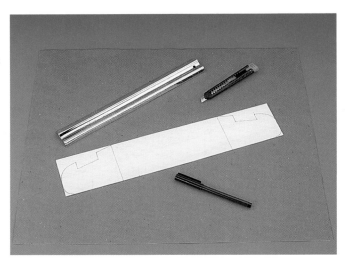

3 Cut around the wing outline, then, using the knife and the metal ruler, cut across the lines separating the wing tips from the center of the wing. Take care to cut only part-way through the wood.

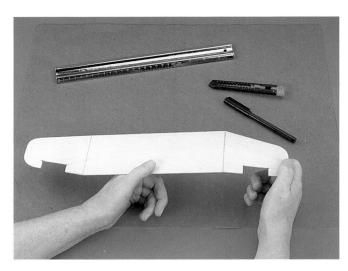

4 Turn the wing over, and gently bend the wing tips up so the wood cracks. Turn the wing over again, and rub cement into the crack.

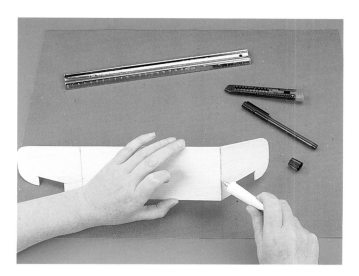

5 Now lie the wing down on the polyethylene sheet spread over your building board, and support the wing tips with matchboxes, pinning the wing into place while the glue dries. When it is thoroughly dry, reinforce the wing joints with strips of gauze bandage attached with PVA glue (see page 12).

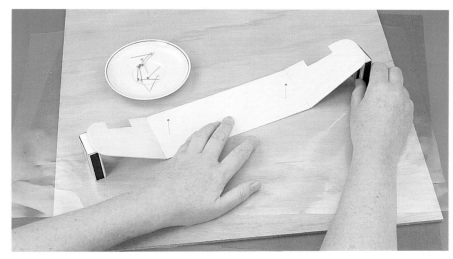

6 Cement the wing into place at the position marked, and reinforce the joint with small triangular balsa fillets. Cut out the tail plane and fins from 1/16″ (1.5mm) balsa, and cement them into place. Use the triangle to make sure that the tail plane is square with the fuselage, and that the fins are glued on at right angles to the tail plane. Use pins to hold them in place while the cement dries.

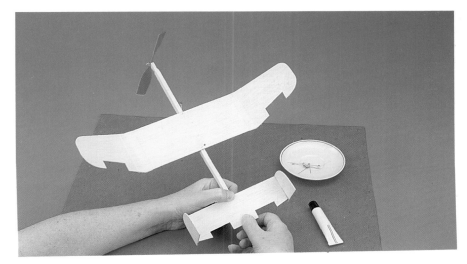

7 Finish the construction by attaching the motor hook. This is made from the paper clip, bent as shown and cut with the pliers.

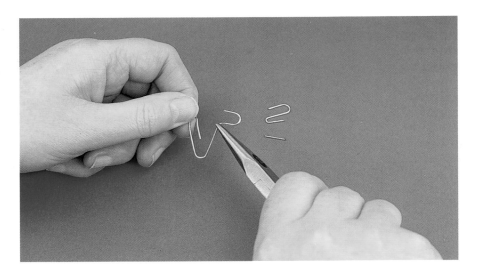

8 Press the end of the clip into the back of the fuselage and secure it with a dab of cement. It will be held in place by the pull of the rubber motor.

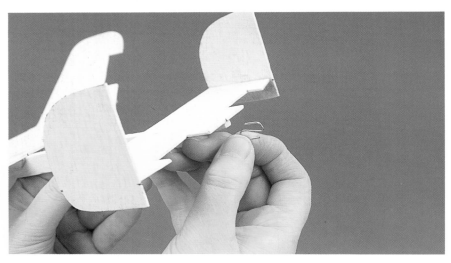

9 Cut a 600mm length of rubber for the motor from a rubber strip 1mm x $\frac{3}{32}''$ (2.5mm). Tie a reef knot in the rubber, and stretch it over the motor hook at the tail then over the hook in the propeller shaft.

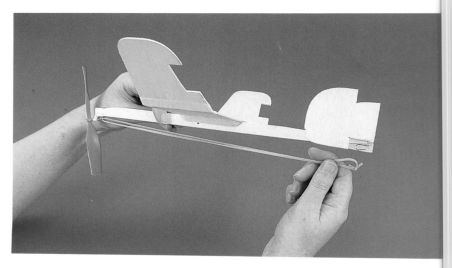

10 Fit the trim tabs to the tail plane and wing, balance the model and try it out by test gliding. Trim it to glide in right-hand circles, as it will fly in left-hand circles under power. Wind the motor by turning the propeller backward (clockwise, looking from the front). Put on about 100 turns for first flights, then gradually increase to not more than 250 turns. You may need to adjust the trim of the model for flight under power.

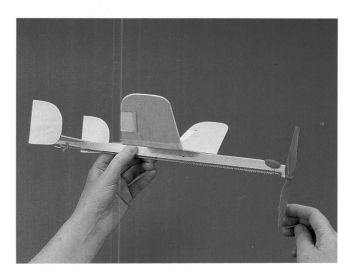

11 The finished model.

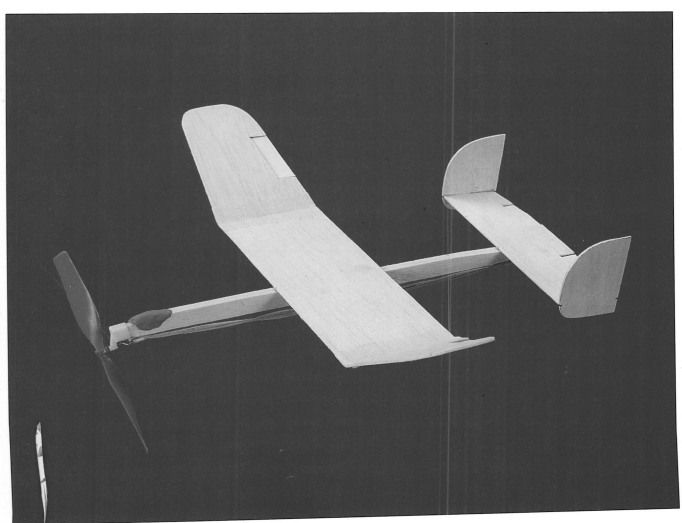

This very simple flying wing will glide surprisingly well. It does not carry the extra weight of a large fuselage and tail plane, so it is very light. Like the Saucerer and Concarde, the trailing edge of the wing is swept up to provide stability.

You will need balsa 1/16" (1.5mm) and 3/16" (4.5mm) thick, a pencil or fine-line marker, a metal ruler, a woodworking knife, sandpaper, tape, dressmaking or modeling pins, a matchbox, and balsa cement.

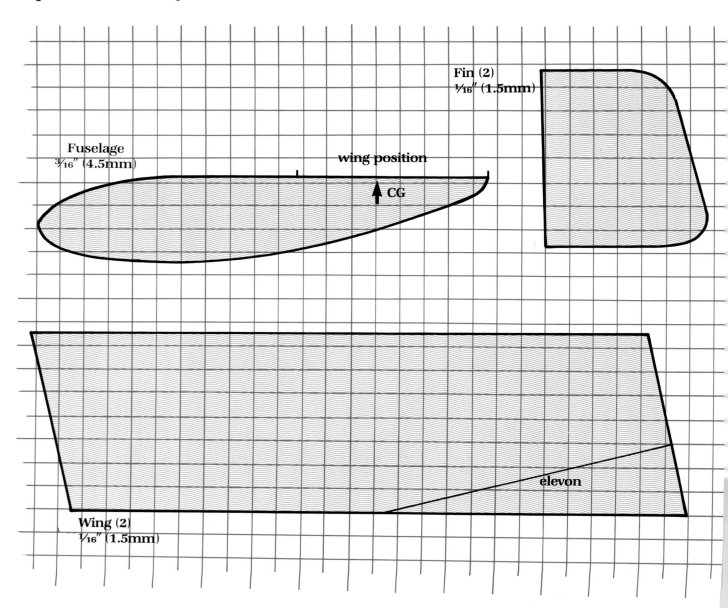

Fin (2)
1/16" (1.5mm)

Fuselage
3/16" (4.5mm)

wing position

CG

Wing (2)
1/16" (1.5mm)

elevon

1 Start by making the wings. These are cut from ¹⁄₁₆" (1.5mm) balsa, and are 280mm long x 75mm wide. The wings are swept back for added stability, and the wing root and wing tips must be cut accurately at an angle of 78°. Tape the wings together temporarily, and lay them flat. Use the ruler to mark the line of the "elevons" (the correct name for the control surfaces of a tail-less aircraft).

2 Cut part-way through the elevons, so they can be bent into the correct position later.

3 Pin down one wing, and support the other wing tip on the matchbox, to provide the correct dihedral angle. Cement the wing joint and pin the wings in position until the cement dries.

4 Mark and cut out the twin fins, and cement them to the wing tips. Do not cement the elevons to the fins yet.

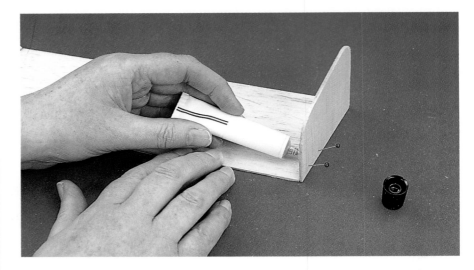

5 Mark and cut out the simple fuselage, then cement the wings into place, reinforcing them with triangular section gussets.

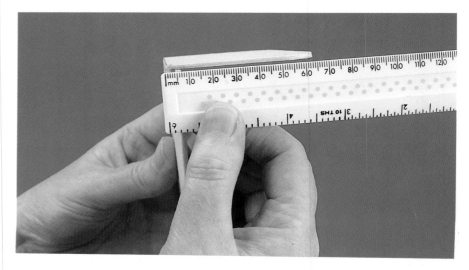

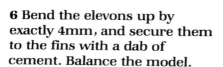

6 Bend the elevons up by exactly 4mm, and secure them to the fins with a dab of cement. Balance the model.

7 Trim and fly the model as for the Saucerer, then cement the elevons permanently in place. This model flies quite slowly, so do not try to launch it too fast.

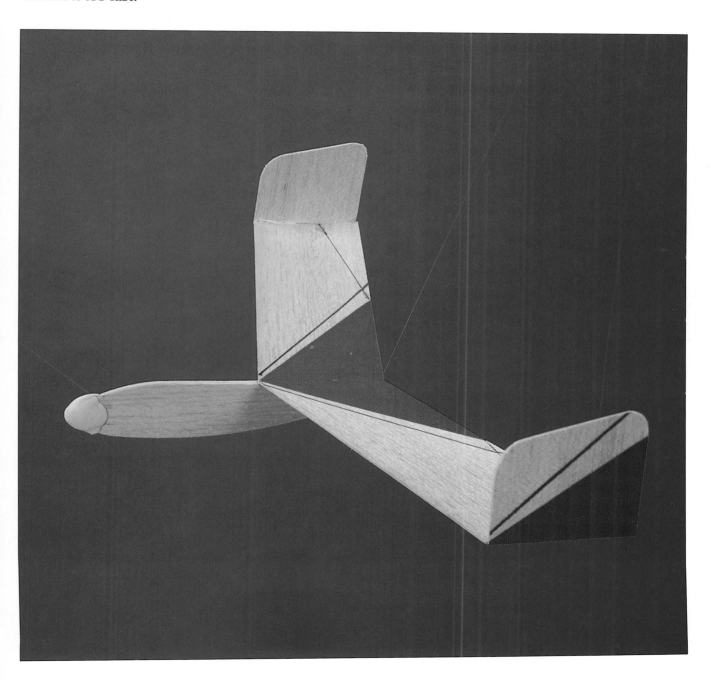

This futuristic shape will probably become familiar, as several full-sized jets are being built in this "canard," or tail-first, design. Canard aircraft are usually very stable in flight and, if properly balanced and trimmed, they will not stall. Starfly is particularly suitable for catapult launching and, with a little ingenuity, you can convert it to rubber power, changing the shape of the nose and attaching the propeller assembly and rubber motor in the same way as for Easy Riser (see pages 29-33).

You will need balsa ¹⁄₁₆″ (1.5mm) and ³⁄₁₆″ (4.5mm) thick, a pencil or fine-line marker, a metal ruler, a woodworking knife, sandpaper, balsa cement, dressmaking or modeling pins, an empty matchbox, a triangle, cardboard, and modeling clay.

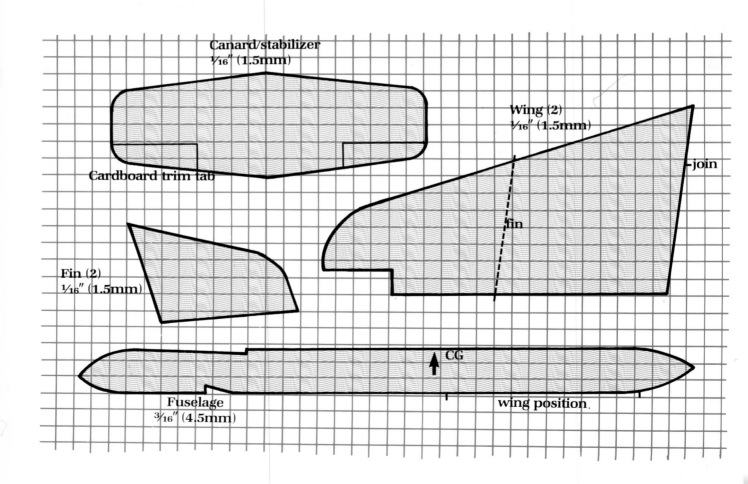

1 Cut the fuselage from ³⁄₁₆″ (4.5mm) balsa, taking special care to make the cutout for the forward wing, or canard surface, very accurately. The depth at the rear of the cut-out should be exactly 2mm.

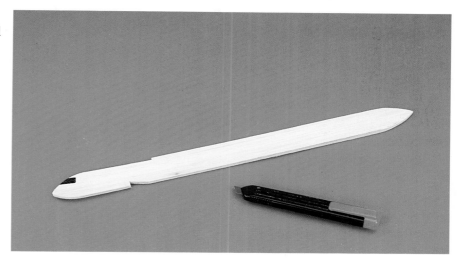

2 Cut the wing, fins, and canard surface from ¹⁄₁₆″ (1.5mm) balsa, making sure that you draw the lines marking the position of the fins on the wing surface. You will probably need to make each wing half from two pieces of balsa sheet, cemented along their edges (see page 11).

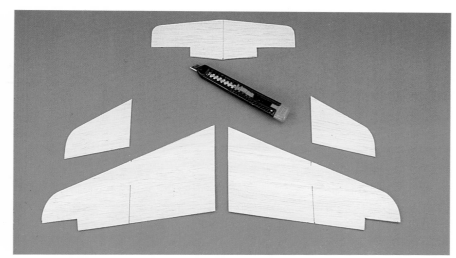

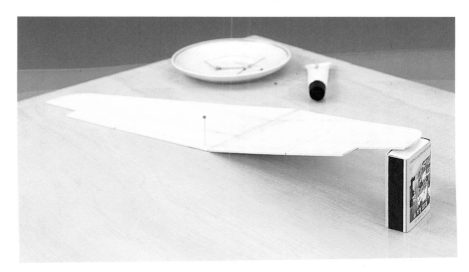

3 Pin down one wing half and cement the other wing half to it, supporting the wing tip with the matchbox to produce the proper dihedral angle.

4 Cement the wings into place, and reinforce the joint where the wing meets the fuselage with short lengths of triangular section balsa stuck to the top of the wing surface. Cement the fins in place on the upper surface of the wings. They should be at 90° to the surface of the wing and, because of the dihedral angle, they will slope inward.

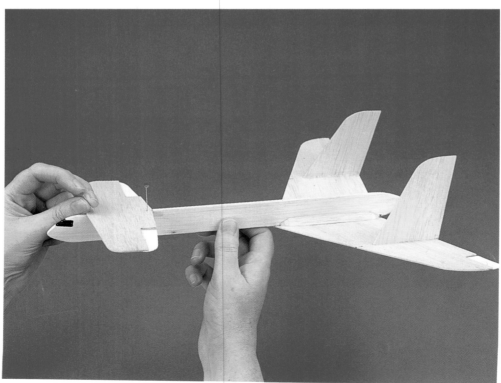

5 Cement the canard, or forward wing, to the front of the fuselage. Attach cardboard trim tabs to the canard and to the tips of the main wing, and balance the model.

6 Trim the model in the usual way but, if the model dives, bend down the trim tab of the front wing to correct it. The center of gravity position is not critical in canards, and you can experiment with moving it backward and forward by adding and removing modeling clay ballast.

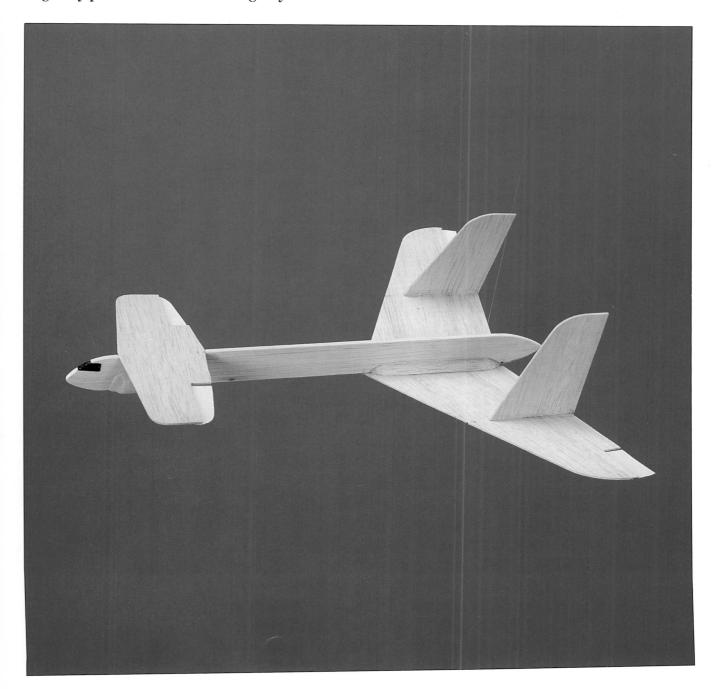

Rhombus

This odd-shaped model flies quite well, but needs careful construction to avoid warps. You will need balsa $\frac{1}{16}''$ (1.5mm) and $\frac{3}{16}''$ (4.5mm) thick, a pencil or fine-line marker, a metal ruler, a woodworking knife, sandpaper, dressmaking or modeling pins, balsa cement, an empty matchbox, and cardboard.

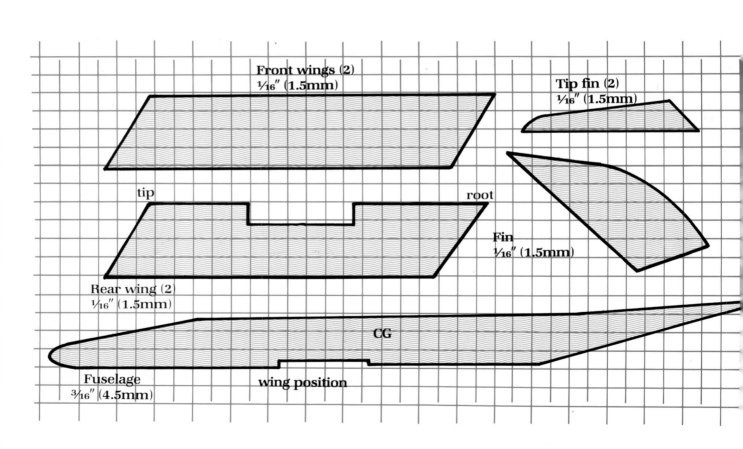

Front wings (2) $\frac{1}{16}''$ (1.5mm)

Tip fin (2) $\frac{1}{16}''$ (1.5mm)

tip

root

Fin $\frac{1}{16}''$ (1.5mm)

Rear wing (2) $\frac{1}{16}''$ (1.5mm)

CG

Fuselage $\frac{3}{16}''$ (4.5mm)

wing position

1 Cut out the fuselage shape from ³⁄₁₆″ (4.5mm) balsa. Shape the rear fuselage carefully, as it determines the angle of the rear wing and so must be accurate.

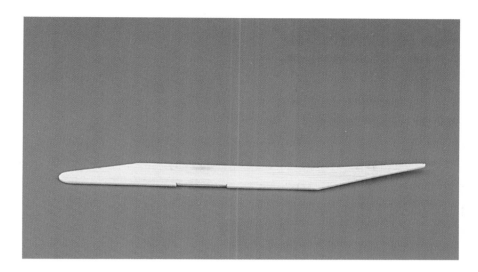

2 Cut out the front and rear wings from ¹⁄₁₆″ (1.5mm) balsa. Note that the angles on the tips and roots of the front wings and on the tips of the rear wings are the same, while the root angle of the rear wings is different. Mark the wings to make sure you don't mix them up.

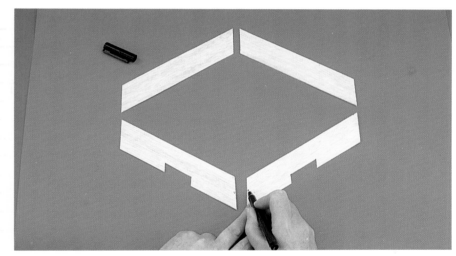

3 Pin down one of the front wings, and cement the other wing half to it. Support this wing tip with the matchbox, to produce the proper dihedral angle.

4 Cement the front wing into the fuselage cutout, making sure that it fits squarely on the fuselage by looking from the front to line it up. Cement the small ¹⁄₁₆″ (1.5mm) tip fins on top of the wing tips.

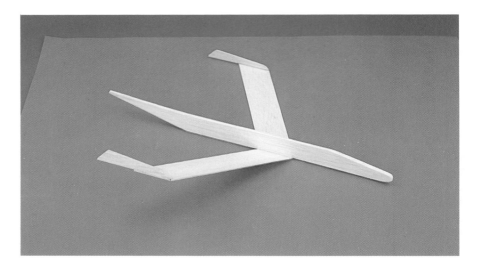

5 Tilt the model over and pin down one wing. Fit the corresponding rear wing into place, so it is positioned under the tip fin and rests on top of the rear of the fuselage. After checking that it fits properly, cement and pin the rear wing into place. Once it has dried thoroughly, repeat the process for the other side. You may need to reshape the root of the rear wings slightly, using sandpaper, so they fit snugly together.

6 If you have assembled the wings correctly, the rear wing will now be twisted slightly upward, producing the same effect as the upswept trailing edge of the Saucerer and Plane Jane models (see pages 21-24 and 34-37). Add the ¹⁄₁₆″ (1.5mm) fin and cement the trim tabs to the center of each rear wing.

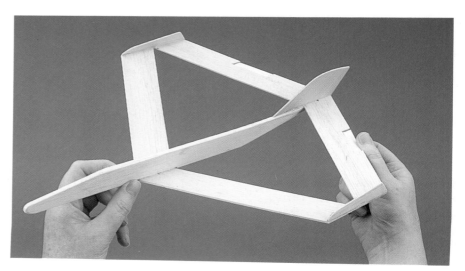

7 Trim the model exactly as for the Saucerer (see pages 21-24), being very careful to position the center of gravity correctly. Because of its complicated shape, this model can break easily if it crashes, so it is not recommended for violent catapult launching.

Helpful hint: If your model has been kept in a damp place, the wings and tail surfaces can become twisted and warped. If this happens, you may be able to straighten them out by twisting them the other way while you dry the wood with hot air from a hair dryer.

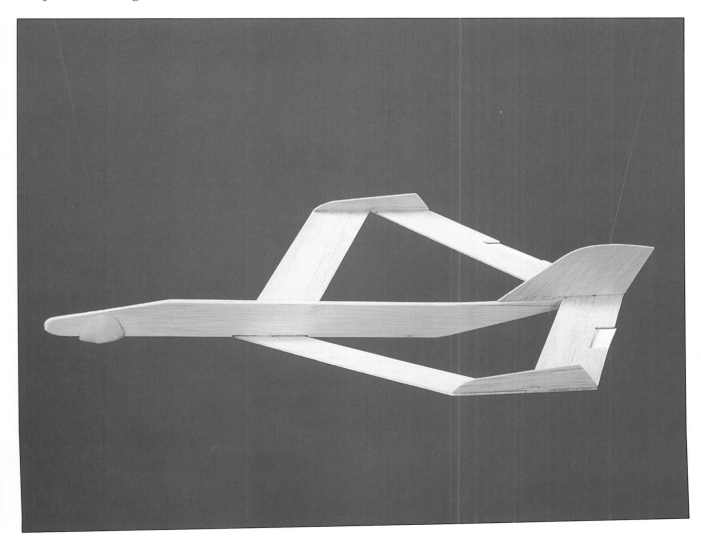

Airfoil
Surface of wing or stabilizer that is curved so as to produce lift as it passes through the air. The simple models in this book have flat wings, which are not so effective in producing lift, but are easier to make.

Ailerons
Control surfaces attached to the wings, which cause an aircraft to roll and help it to turn.

Airplane
Any form of aircraft that is supported in flight by wings.

Balsa wood
Very light South American wood used for constructing models.

Canard
A "tail-first" aircraft, which has the wing at the back and the stabilizer at the front. If properly built and balanced, it is very stable in flight.

Cement
A special glue used to bond balsa wood. It dries quickly and is quite strong.

Center of gravity
Balance point of an aircraft. A correct center of gravity is very important for stability in flight.

Control surface
Movable flap that controls the flight path of an aircraft.

Dihedral
The angle by which the two halves or outer parts of the wing are raised above the horizontal.

Downthrust
Technique in which the propeller is tilted down so as to prevent the aircraft from climbing too steeply under power.

Elevator
Movable surface attached to the stabilizer, which causes an aircraft to climb or dive.

Elevons
Control surface on a tail-less, delta-winged or flying saucer type of aircraft, which combines the function of elevators and ailerons.

Fillet
Small triangular length of wood used to reinforce a joint. Balsa cement can also be used to make a fillet.

Fin
Fixed vertical surface at the rear of an aircraft, which helps it to fly in a straight line.

Fuselage
The "body" of an aircraft.

Incidence
Angle at which wings are tilted above the center line of the aircraft, helping them to generate lift.

Leading edge
The front edge of a wing, stabilizer or fin.

Rudder
Control surface attached to the fin, which helps an aircraft to turn.

Stabilizer
Flying surface which tends to hold the wing at the correct position to produce lift for flight. In conventional aircraft, the stabilizer or tail plane is at the back; in canards, it is at the front.

Stability
Ability of an aircraft to fly steadily.

Stall
Condition in which the wings suddenly cease to produce lift. In a model, a stall usually follows a climb, when the model loses speed and dips its nose sharply, recovering then stalling again, to produce a series of swoops.

Trailing edge
The rear of a wing, stabilizer or fin.

Trim tab
Small movable flap attached to a flying surface, which can be used to make small adjustments to the flight path and to correct the trim.

Warp
Twist in a wing or control surface, which interferes with normal flight.

Wing
The main lifting surface supporting an aircraft in flight.

Organization

Academy of Model Aeronautics
1810 Samuel Morse Drive
Reston, VA 22090
(703) 435-0750

Promotes modeling as a recognized sport; answers inquiries.

Books to read

Berliner, Don. *Flying-Model Airplanes.* Minneapolis, MN; Lerner, 1982.

Berliner, Don. *Scale-Model Airplanes.* Minneapolis, MN; Lerner, 1982

Throsteinn, Kristinsson. *Balsa Wood Projects.* New York; Sterling, 1988.

McNeil, M. J. *The KnowHow Book of Flying Models*, Tulsa, OK; EDC, 1977.

PRINTED IN BELGIUM BY
proost
INTERNATIONAL BOOK PRODUCTION